Easy words to read

Fox on a box

Phil Roxbee Cox

Illustrated by Stephen Cartwright

Edited by Jenny Tyler

Language consultant:

Marlynne Grant

BSc, CertEd, MEdPsych, PhD, AFBPs, CPsychol

There is a yellow duck to find on every page.

First published in 2003 by Usborne Publishing Ltd. Usborne House, 83-85 Saffron Hill, London EC1N 8RT, England. www.usborne.com

Copyright ©2003 Usborne Publishing Ltd.

Hungry Fox spots
a box.

Hungry Fox hops onto the box.

He tries to reach...

3

Hungry Fox pushes the box.

"Now I'm as tall as the wall!" calls Fox.

SPLAT!

Hungry Fox
is on the box.

"I can reach
the cooling
pies!" cries
Fox.

But Pup and
Fat Cat ...

PRIZE

...put a stop to that.

Hungry Fox falls
into the box.

He heaves
himself out...

15

"I'm back in the box!"

shouts Happy Fox.